PERSEVERE

From a Schizoaffective Mind:

Poetry, Prose, and Thoughts
of a U.S. Army Veteran

By Daniel Nepveux

- DEDICATION -

This collection is dedicated to the voiceless and hopeless. Those who spend their entire lives hidden in the dark, wanting only to stop feeling.

But I want ya'll to know that it's okay to feel what you do.

You don't have to hide in that darkness alone. And I know you're there because I can hear you. We share the same night, so let's talk.

- FORWARD -

I have spent my entire life feeling shit. Ever since I can remember I've been a sensitive human being. I got my feelings hurt constantly and never quite learned how to voice my pain in a healthy manner. Then, even in sleep, I would battle with some unseen threat. Eventually my nightmares became part of my waking truth and I found myself sick with worry constantly. That my mom would die in her sleep or that my monsters would take my little brother.

And so I spent most of my childhood praying and yearning for a way to become strong and tough to better defend myself.

Eventually it happened and I became able to play the sports where I was now knocking people down instead of the other way round.

After high school I went straight into the infantry constantly trying to make myself into a weapon in hopes that I wouldn't have to be afraid anymore.

Well even that failed and in my young adulthood I found myself scared.

All the time.

Terrified.

Eventually I began writing down my fears and my thoughts and I found ways to transcribe my waking nightmares into something understandable.

This book of poems and writings has been collected over the past few years, during one of the darkest descents into madness that I had yet experienced.

I hope you enjoy the read and may be gain insight into a troubled mind.

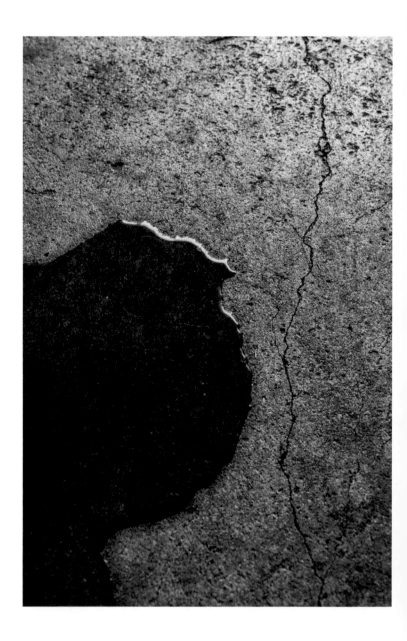

BLACK SCARS

I'd always thought
them to be
battle scars
of
Triumphs past
but now I know
a painful truth
that each stitched
scar
would forecast

My bleeding heart
It's flesh torn back
beautiful fountains
of blinding red
But I never knew
of why I was
not once asking
of how I bled

And to see it now
with such clarity
a shining moth
against the glass
of translucent tears
that shape its fall
buried beneath
the
blackened grass

LAY BESIDE ME

Lay beside me
please stay till morning.
These dark hours
of loveless doubts
were not meant to weather alone.
I have not hope,
nor light for guidance
But in your presence
I find in me
a quiet strength I'd not known.
I beg to Love
and wish for thee'
Yet dreams come masked
with dark intent,
ill shadows of severed Bones.
So wake not now,
but rest till light;
let lashes kiss
bare cheeks of rose
under white sheets of precious
stone.
STILL I fail
and reach to hold,
one desperate need
to grasp and wrap
Tears open wounds that should
have known....
My dream spread wings,
away it'd flown.
My Always Failure
I am Alone.

ROYAL AND RED

I would have broken walls
gladly walked through stone

But You...

You built a fortress
I could not scale
and hid my redemption
behind your throne

And so
My wounds
continually bled

this unraveling
thread
of the
strength we bred

Crowned
useless
Royal
And
Red

STAY WITH ME

I've imagined this night
countless times as
infinite moments
sharing the same world
As my life flows
over my arm
it rains onto the ground
feeding the netherworld
I've poisoned my heart
it cries out in anguish
as my breaths
grow silent
My mind is racing
thirty four years of memories
play pictures
and flash by cold and violent
Now ghostly figures
of wisping whispers
approach and grab my
weakened form
Stay with me
they say
stay with me
but how can I
when my spirit is deformed?
Sharply they retort
stay with me
and a crushing blow
shocks my eyes
open and there is light
too bright and assaulting
I can see my life
devoid of hope or strength
I settle in for the long night
stay with me
stay with me
stay with me

THE DISTANT DRUMS

It's not a question of whether we break or not...
It's a game of wear and tear.
There is nothing that can stand the relentless
march of time.
But instead of rain and rivers cutting through
the earth over thousands of years;
It's our tears and cries of grief, cutting through
US over thousands and thousands of moments.
Each one a perfect puncture of our
vulnerable hearts.
When does enough become enough?
Can't we all feel it?
That distant drum that plays out
our predestined beats?
What if we don't want to dance anymore?
I can hear it now.
Here and now.
But I no longer recognize the song,
nor hum its melody beneath my breath.
What choice do we really have?
Can you still hear it?
Pulling your feet with the dreadful current of
expectations and shame?
The drums play on and we all still dance.
But I wonder.....
Does the music stop if I decide to sit?

CHILD'S GAME

Ring-a-round the roses,
A pocket full of posies,
Ashes! Ashes!
We all fall down
and down
and down
and down

CONSTANT CONFLICT

This life of constant Conflict
caught and held taught
within lines of dispute
his nature fights his welfare
A millennia of contradiction
how can he live
when life is but poisonous
breaths of conscious despair
Now what of hope?
These dreams ascend to hell
and descend through laughing clouds
of confinement
To climb this tower
of vague promise and peace
he must abandon his powers
and embrace refinement
How can he convey
the loneliness and uncertainty
of the solitary desolation
wrought from Heartache
Where the moon has turned
and her dark side,
a reminder of infinite nights
to blanket day break
Abandon the thought
that practiced mages
may turn off the dark
with your surrender
Or graciously give
freedom
in exchange
for stability and quiet splendor

THE LIGHTHOUSE

I've seen these streets before.
The same low hanging branches,
stripped of their vibrant colors, exude no life.
The road bears the same cracks that reveal the
scars inflicted over years of endless wondering.
I don't want to do this.
These shoes have traveled endless miles
and now are worn to nothing
but scraps of futility.
I don't want to do this now.
Just when I can finally see the stars again.....
They hide in unison.
Flirtatiously teasing absolution and acceptance;
yet always out of reach.
Instead the skies assault me with storms too
powerful to bear upon my burdened shoulders
anymore.
I don't want to do this again.
Buried beneath the ageless horrors of past
fears I suffocate from their relentless weight.
They press.
They bear down.
They engulf me.
I can't do this.
But still....
I wake and rise.

I'M TIRED

I'm tired of waking up.

Of counting the hours until I can try to sleep again.
I'm tired of knowing that every single day
will usually be worse in some way.

I'm tired of seeing infinite darkness
and emptiness for my future.

I'm tired of begging for help.
I'm tired of being the burden others bear.
I'm tired of being endlessly and constantly confused.

Of never being able to remember anything.
Of not knowing what to trust as "real".

I'm tired of my nightmares being my reality.
Of having to experience that terror and horror daily.

I'm tired of hating myself and everything I am.
I'm tired of dropping and breaking shit.
I'm tired of being the absolute failure.
I'm tired of being terrified of eye contact.
Of knowing they want me done and gone.

I'm tired of battling minute to minute,
and second to second,
just to stay alive and keep some tiny loose
grip on my sanity.

I'm tired of wondering what happiness is.
Of watching time crawl by in mockery of me.
I'm tired of hearing
and experiencing false moments.
Of having to wonder if it's real, or just me.
I'm tired of being tired.
I'm tired of being me.

INFINITE BREATHS

Sometimes this endless loop of perceived anguish
is met by an equally persistent second wind;

that carries us forward regardless of our pain.

It is our Infinite Wind.

THEY ARE GLASS

I am but glass
A darkened reflection
Of misconception
And forever smiles
Of feverish strain
I stand atop
My mountain of loss
A lonely Kingdom
Of growing regret
The world broken and stained
Heed not these cries
Of tortured deception
Their substitute joy
Will feast on your hopes
Leaving you broken and chained
I see but glimpses
As through a mirror
Of fictitious fog
And whimsical ghosts
That cannot be sustained
My past
My dreams
My loved are lost
Beaten, Bloody, and Pained

ALL WE WERE

Hello my dearest lost and loved
I'd thought you gone for certain
of
Fallen, Broken, Shattered stone
from unkept graves upon your bones
Now and Always
Overgrown
Simply forever
You alone.

Never forgotten yet Left Behind
All we once were intertwined
A path of Tombs together sewn
Leads countless victims to unknown's
Scorched in hell
Lives dethroned
Sulfur, Brimstone
Yet still...alone.

How did you do it?
Make me understand!
Why you laid waste to every last strand
Making you precious, a light to be shone
Instead of Buried, Bygone, Blotted...
Disowned
Forever Destined
To shuffle and Roam
Not quite Dead
But always...
Alone.

August 9, 2017

"Sometimes I think we forget just how dangerous being alive is and how incredibly breakable we are. I'm not saying be scared, but I am saying don't assume everything is going to be okay tomorrow. Try not to take for granted what you think is a given. That includes your health, your safety, your family, your opportunities, your security, your loved ones, your dreams, ect. ect. ect. And I know it easier to think you're right and that you have all the answers.....but the simple truth of the matter is that none of us know very much at all. So may be be more aware of your surroundings. Pay attention. Say I'm sorry. Be open to the possibility that you're wrong. Don't assume you have all the time in the world to do or say something. Go on that trip. Punch your boss in the face. Do or say something that you think you could just do or say tomorrow. Because the truth is......sometimes people aren't around the next day. Sometimes that job you were going to apply for is snatched up by someone else. And sometimes that lightening strike does hit someone."

-Daniel

MISSING

Hello Daniel,
How are you?

Well...
Day by day
and in-between
I stalk an elusive
and silent dream.

Now...
what could it be
that you stubbornly seek?
Some magic spell
to awaken your heart?
Or something instead
you wish to depart?

No, nothing like that
You're thinking too hard
It's something to cherish
something to hold
A relic of warmth
that favors the bold

Hell, I've got it!
So no cheating or retreating
if I get this right.
I'll start with reflections
a black to your white
You said Day.....
So Night after Night
Wrapped in darkness you cope
Wanting and waiting
For that Fucking
HOPE

THE BELLS

When they sound
they must be found
or suffer their promise to be
But listen not
if they're never sought
those pleas shall drown at sea
Yet came they too late
those cries of fate
to save him from his doom
He had fallen far
below his scars
to the steps of an empty Room.
And with a roar
he kicked down its door
hoping answers hidden there
But hark instead
a bodiless head
above an empty chair
The man cried out
and turned about
then came to a sudden halt
From the walls fixture
a mirrored picture
hung laughing at his faults
Mirrors on mirrors
all shedding tears
covered the weeping walls
T'was his own ghost
without its host
wailing the crow's call

THEY STARE

They stare
Cold and Insidious
Bent ever on my destruction
Relentless
They stab and slash
a transition of my self-induction
To this aching fever
and gentle rawness
of tormenting tenderness
A raging wound
bleeding unmotivated pain
into a state of endlessness
False prophet
False Face
They chant unknowingly his name
For though they mean
to mock, meddle, and maketh' misery
They've foolishly played his game
And now
through swirling squares
Of shaking circles
I see new
And haunting
chains of skulls in purple
Dancing up
My scarred arms
these maps of terror
show me the depths
of which I sink
And future hells to bare

OUR GHOSTLY DANCE

This is the Empty
a canvas of
extraordinary vacant meaning
idle and vain
We dance above
arms outstretched
and hands held tight
as our ghosts circle
oblivious to our pain
Does no one see?
The splashes of color
that rain from
our translucent ballet?
Toes dip and tickle
leaving such beautiful
vibrant silhouettes
the forever display
The story of all
and each to come
bound by fate
our flickers and shimmers
pirouette as one
And together they paint
with perfect abandon
until one falls
and burns the sky
their dance finally done

FALSE FACES OF TRINITY

Climb higher.
Cut deeper.
Do more.
Can you hear them?
Whispers carried on a breeze,
cold and senseless.
How do you push on?
when you feel them tear through?
talons and claws stretched out from below; deeper
than dirt and beyond the draped curtains of darkness.
They grab you.
Tearing through flesh,
in a blooded baptism of fire.
You try to scream
but are drowned out by laughter,
as angels drape a tear stained noose
around your neck.
You are dying.
Bleeding out in a demon's pit of bubbling tar,
as winged blessings choke you
in fits of delighted madness.
So you try and fight.

But how do you win without conviction?
How do you persevere without strength?
But your questions come too late.
The time has come.
And in this last desperate plea for help
you take your final breath.
But your hands rise to your face
against your will;
forcing your mouth open,
stretching till it breaks
and hangs low by its skin.
And from your own shadows
come all the doubts and pain.
Standing before you
they grin and savor their victim;
with lust and a depraved hunger
to feed you their fill.
From their wicked hands,
they pour a bitter chalk
down your searing throat;
where it Burns
Butchers
and Poisons everything you ever were.
And so....
In thoughts
forever silenced
you become your wish.

A CHILD'S DREAM

I saw a man
in my room last night
then he was gone
at first light
I saw him twice more
throughout the day
always watching
not a word to say
When I got home
He was there inside
He stabbed me once
And then I died

TODAY BLEEDS

Today as tomorrow now as one
An unwelcome shadow slipped silently
into the segway of my heart
and there laid sooted roots
of endless despair.
The night's tide now bleeds
Drowning the sand in it's flood
How can I swim,
whilst my soul is weighted
with wretched stones from nowhere
Breathe baby breathe
Her mantra whispers delicately in my ear
As my arms waste
To stand afloat in this mud of blackened sin
Where is the moon
To tame this tide of wicked false promises
My feet dance and cramp
reaching for the bottom
Not a question of if I find it
But when

WE IN THE GARDEN

In gardens we wait
  while tears dampen our soil
  desolate now
  and withered with age

Timeless our hearts
  Watch stone walls crumble
  Distancing warmth
  As we quietly rage

Is it definite then?
  We're all strangers again?
  Left only with
  memories
  that number too few?!

Because I cannot see!
  This looking glass blurs
  My smile
  Death's ghost
  Life's Tenderness too!

What can we do?
　　Was not hope to Renew?
　　That which was broken...
　　That which was through?

So we in the garden
　　Will collect our grief's water
　　And fill to the brim
　　Our wishing well

Knowing we tend
　　with the slow
　　burn of regret
　　an empty bed
　　Where we now dwell

And each of us listens
　　for their own paragon
　　a barren lullaby
　　a mournful dove

Sung in verse
　　our simple truth
　　We are
　　Lovers with naught to Love

THE STAND

Why did you come
And knock down the door
These rooms were full
No space to spare
Yet still you came
And broke my heart

No warning at all
And no time to prepare
You tore and ripped
Slashed and bashed
Leaving us crippled in parts

I still can't see
Your shape, it shifts
from terror
to horror and back
Such vivid destruction
on souls you wrought
mutilated, damaged, and
racked

Beyond the grave
They whisper with thought
"Come to Me
I yearn not for love
Just peace,
so grasp my hand"
Then screaming with rage
they clamor and clap
So desperate
I make my stand

TO FEAR MYSELF

I fear the Devoutly Desire
for Deliverance
that implausibly echoes from the future.
The Preposterous
false Promise
of a Peace obtained
through a mélange
of ruinous obsessions
to self-immolation.

INTIMATE FAMILIARITY

The more intimate our familiarity with the darkest parts of ourselves...
The more manageable, and less terrifying, our relationship with them will be.
We each know how truly all-encompassing a state of futility and hopelessness can be.
How the world around you becomes a stark and colorless hell on earth; where your screams for help fall upon deaf ears, and the relentless wheels of time continue turning without sparing you a single thought.
We don't want to know this place.
But unfortunately, that is not for us to decide.
And sometimes......
The best thing we CAN do is embrace this part of ourselves, and greet it as an old friend.

The more intimate
and familiar
to the darkest
parts of me
The more understood
and less terrifying
my life with them
will be
As Stars to Dust
I am my shadow
and every smile
You see
So set and destined
to be the sum
of my fears,
laughs, terrors,
And glee.

MIRRORED DREAMS

I used to dream
  of what I'd found
  in every minute
  of wakeful sleep.

A journey of
  such helpless wonder
  still waters running
  ever deep.

The dreams were not
  of what could be
  nor aimless hopes
  of fractured fiction.

They were instead
  my waking truths
  seamless
  without confliction.

How lucky then
  was I in life?
  Days mirrored
  what dreams had meant

Yet so foolish
  to have missed
  the sickness
  despairing descent.

HEAVEN'S MEADOW

It may not have been mine
But under my care
This Meadow Blossomed
with
Songs soft and fair

Trapped, my heart still is here

Find its smear
That I fear rots near

Left in Heaven's Meadows tears.

July 25, 2017

"And just when you think you are starting to get a grasp on things.....Nature comes tearing through your life like a hurricane with the last thing you would expect or want. So now you're back to one day at a time again."

-Daniel

WHY?

How could any of this be right?
I can't understand these words
Or their hidden meaning
I'm holding on to this rope
My lifeline to the world
Tears and blood streaming
This mortal sin of life
Holds me against the cliffs
With no holds to grasp
How am I here?
Why am I here?
Do I let go and breathe that last gasp

CONSTANT CONFLICT II

These walls are my home, prison, and palace
 Walk these stone corridors
 And witness the love and malice
 Cracked, weathered, in crumbling
 They speak to me through gaps
 Taunting my life and tumbling
 Winding stairs that creak and groan
 Impossibly infinite in their open tower
 I make my way through the darkened tone
 Stop these steps to my predestined fall
 Grab these iron rails and hold myself
 From doing the same thing to lose it all
 Hold up my hands to my face
 Screaming and curdling to these bars of steel
 How do I slow down this pace
 Which leads to my own six foot space

A LOVE NOTE

Is love but blind allegiance
or bonds of unspoken caliber
wisps of forgotten moments
painted with bones
on boards of white

You are my beautifully perfect
personal siren of infinite kindness;
with no killing joke to foul the cure.
And I, the luckiest man on earth
to be so privileged as to be loved by you
and to love you.
You are my everything.

ONE FINALITY

Twelve feet below
and infinitely removed
It's real....
It's Not....

Consumed
Subdued
and bruised

A single silent moment
Shared with death
Down to it now

One last breath.

THIS BLADE'S LIGHT

Don't act so damned surprised
The darkness of this life
Has hastily grabbed all control
And with it the roadmaps
And secret passages of lightened love
To your heart black as coal
How then to rid it
From your soul's toll
Of flashpoint pains
This blade of deliverance
Glistens with the stars blood
as each droplet falls with the light's rain
Please remember this
This dark moment
should sear into being
These pre-scars outline
Each attempt to gain dominance
Over the demon's fleeing

"Death must be so beautiful. To lie in the soft brown earth, with the grasses waving above one's head, and listen to silence. To have no yesterday, and no to-morrow. To forget time, to forget life, to be at peace."

—Oscar Wilde, The Canterville Ghost

THE QUIET ONES

We are the quiet ones.
Those whispered dying breaths,
frozen in a drifting fog.
There and gone
with each passing beat
of our failing hearts.
Gasping for life
in a world made bare
of empathy and love.
We desperately reach
for hands to grab hold of,
finding instead
clenched fists and hate.
And then it sounds,
splitting the night sky.
Bells and Drums
tolling our bitter end.
And so we fade
into the forgotten,
passing on
our invisible suffering.
This world demands payment
for our jubilant laughter,
and so our pain must pass
to someone after.
Understand and remember
that all must balance
And when we reach out
with open hands for love,
our struggles will remember
those clenched hands of loathing.

THE END OF THE ROAD

How softly we walk
on this cobbled crumbling stone
one foot leading another
Lost in the unknown
Yet if we were to gather
the courage to peek beyond
We might still be delivered
to our light as it dawns
So seek not deliverance
from your darkness and pain
but instead push through
And emerge once again

FOR YOU

To see you
One more time
Is all I wish of this
The whole thing
Every second
Anything to feel your kiss

Were we made
To see it all
Or just to glimpse the infinite
Would it be
Too beautiful
Too true and definite

For tonight
I'll sit with you
That you may hear my song
And may you
Sleep as quick
As my heart does long

For you

"I wanted to write down exactly what I felt,
but somehow the paper stayed empty;
and I could not have described it any better."

- WTM

THE CALL OF IT ALL

Call it wandering
Or call it lost
I'm on my way back
To where it all started
No more faces in the dark
or ghostly apparitions of past failures
Backtracking I climb
Having forgotten how far I fell
Where to my body was carted
Surrounded by flowing green moss
I am breathless
The smell of the sea assaults me
And I remember everything
Hovering in mid air as I fell
The dreadfully beautiful jagged rocks
racing towards me
Try to feel one last emotion
But I don't feel anything
Only the empty of my life

BEAR UNTIL YOU BREAK

I am and I feel
  every minuscule moment

yet still somehow drowning
  in this perilous pool

Of shapeless spirits dancing
  in the dying of the light

casting only cruelty
  with intent to destroy

And as their shadows grow
  extending ever closer

the outstretched hands
  grasp for my throat

Wanting and desperate now
  they pull me in with them

for a dance I never got
  to the song I never wrote

I AM

I am a memory.
Lift me in your arms
And remember me
For how I was
Before these shallow depths
Of silent cries
Christened countless cons of misery
I am a smile
Remember my story
And reconcile
The boy who whispered
And his anguished wails
That weaved witchly warnings of blackened bile
I am a vicious and vanquished villain
of no validity.
I am a negative.
A nameless narrator of Naught.
I am Nothing.

THE DREAM THAT SAVED REALITY
 Are there still footprints on the moon?

A Dream that saved my life ....
   I experienced a very very rapid and deadly decline of my health; and complete respiratory failure.....
which resulted in me being life flighted to a respiratory specialist hospital that staffed a Pulmonologist.
I had been put under sedation almost within only ten minutes of first arriving at my small town emergency room, for not being able to breathe.
They put me under and then it was life flight time.
   I truly had not a single moment to pause things for even a second to reach out and tell anyone at all what was happening; not even half a micro-moment to say 'I Love You' to anyone before being put into an oblivion hell of a seemingly never ending suspended animation.
  Some of the delirium and disturbing hallucinations were unspeakably horrifying and unpleasant....
So inexplicably wrong, and unthinkable, in their insults against every single law of nature and God.....that I will NEVER speak or write of them......
EVER.

   I never should have made it through.....
   I never should have been able to   unconsciously feel your prayers and love through the darkness I was in.....
   And I never should have survived.....

   But I'm starting to believe that I may be in each of yalls debts; for every loving thought, prayer, and hope....
Because I think ya'll kept me alive through sheer Love and Will. Thank you you so much for the support and I love y'all.

   But there was at least one kind and beautiful hallucination, during the hell of 16-17 days of being ventilated in a coma hell. And after getting better I thought back on it and realized something that almost brought me to tears like a little school boy baby bitch.

So while still in the comatose state, I had yet to respond to any stimulus or prompts from the doctors; but they meds they had me on had my brain in absolute overdrive with VERY REAL AND CLEAR really weird and messed up dreamlines.

Anyhow....there was one dreamline that is still very clear to me.

I am laying in a lone hospital bed in the ICU....

The Room has caught fire and there is smoke everywhere.....

But standing next to me in my bed was my father holding my hand but staring straight ahead refusing to look at me.

I urge him to please open the elevator so that we can get out of there....

But he ignores me so I ask him another 2 or 3 times..... finally getting an answer....

" I'm sorry son but I can't help unless you squeeze my hand..."

So I squeeze his hand a few times.

He then smiles and says, "that's all you needed to do", and suddenly we were off the floor and the dream moved on.

Well it turns out the Very first time I ever responded to stimuli, and showed that I might decide to live, was when the doctor held my hand and put the phone to my ear and my father begged me over the phone to squeeze the doctors hand....and I did.

Anyhow take what you will from this story....

Either way I am relearning just how short and precious life can be, And I am so thankful to have you guys as my friends and to have had your love and support.

Thank you so much.

ROTTING

I am laced with rotting veins
Each more winding and more evident than the last
How did it come to this?
Was it my predestined future or past
Either way I am dying
And amongst the tall grass my body sinks
into a twirling sunken grave of mud and tears
I have but to accept this glass of poison and drink
And all pain shall dissipate
Into a gust of shadowed wind and smoke
The release into the gaping mouth of absolution
And wrapped in it's feverish and silk-lined cloak

FALLING

I remember
 what it's like to fly.
 How the wind
 holds you up
 and kisses your cheeks.
 But I forgot
 how to laugh
 and trust to try
 How to embrace the empty beneath.
 My chute
 was tangled and
 I dropped for ages
 Through cloud, ice, and rain
 Falling and Failing
 with shattered Splinters
 bone, silence, and pain.
 I knew that I should try
 and move.
 But who wants to
 slither and crawl?
 When for
 seasons they've run,
 flown and soared
 over every trying squall?

"I don't want to kill anybody.
I just don't like bullies....
doesn't matter where they're from."

- Captain America

DIFFERENT IS DANGEROUS

They are not to live
But only to exist
Upon their love of HATRED
Towards any in their midst
Who differ in mindset
Intelligence, looks, and life
Hurling insults and being mean
Stabbing with words for their knives

LIFE

I stand in this forest of mystery as the Sun
breaks through the leaves and bathes it's ground.
In its light I am reminded that there is beauty
to this world to appreciate and love.
As I lift my head to the light I feel its warmth
and the promise of a possible personal future
that contains life; and perhaps even joy.
Something I've not felt in too long to count.

I continue my walk in thought.
Grateful for the rustling of the trees
as a cold breeze kisses my cheeks as it passes.
Is this life?
Have I been so blind as to shut myself into
eternal darkness till the end of my days?
Or is there still time?
Time to reach out and hold someone.
Time to breathe in the essence of life.
Time to live?
Is there still time?

"Once more into the fray,
into the last good fight I'll ever know. Live and
die on this day, live and die on this day."

-The Grey

I WISH

I wish that this all was as easy as making a decision.
As simple as choosing to be what we want to be.
Happy.
Hopeful.
Joyful.
And Driven.
To be free of these binding shackles of personal
suffering.
To erase the branding that seared permanent loss
and self loathing into your very being.
How grand could life be....
If by singular thought, you had the power to shift
and change the fabric of your destiny?
Just by "making" the choice to be....
Happy.
But this is not in our control, and nothing so simple
can flip our fortunes.
Yet...
Although we have not the powers to WILL
our desperate desires into existence...
We Do have the fortitude and strength to WILL
ourselves to FIGHT for that aspired utopia.
We may not reach the constellations we strive for...
But as long as we hold faith and maintain our course
through each and every battle....
We stand at least a chance to win our cause.
Because that's what you're fighting for...
Your Life.
And though we did not ask to be drafted into this war;
We CAN choose to fight.
We CAN choose to care.
And we CAN choose to claw, bleed, and roar our
way through this monstrous and terrifying war.
We can at least try one more time.
One more fight.
Once more into the fray.

HE AND ME

He's there for all to see.
But none bother,
Only me.
The clicks of his hoofed feet
Mark his distance,
My Retreat.
Where will it lead for he?
There's not room here,
Not for me.

July 28, 2017

"I have this dream, where I'm walking through the wilderness on the side of a mountain. It keeps getting steeper and steeper and the brush keeps getting thicker and thicker. But there is no sense of urgency like I'm running from something or trying desperately to get to the top. Just a never ending hike upwards. Constantly being snagged and cut by dead wood and branches. On and on and on I climb. I keep expecting the vegetation to get shorter or for the sun to finally break through the forest canopy, but it never happens. And it never really ends. I climb until I wake, never making any progress."

-Daniel

THE CONSUMPTION OF THE CONSTANT

I want to consume this darkness
Swallow it whole and for good
But it evades my grasp and mocks me
From the windows of my broken mind
My body is covered with weeping scars
I don't what to do with 'em all
I thought I could stand and defend my ground
But there's no strength left to find
I get sick to my stomach when I see it
While it circles my mind out of reach
A ghost of my past and lonely future
What if everyone I know leaves me
I'm trapped here and lost for weeks
What can I do to release my mind
And heart together as one
Finally opened to the world and free

SIRENS CALL

I'm seeking answers
but none will come
how empty this thoughtless void
where no rhyme may break it's seal
Instead these echoes
will ferment and foul
for hours and ages
each drop of fate
falls unable to feel
I am trapped
and cannot stir
no wind nor current
to push this keel
to set a lifeless sail
And under its surface
the waters beneath
a bottomless mouth that waits in malice
to strike the coffins nail
So struck its promise
to homeless hearts
I have but to embrace its fold
and worries shall be no more
How tempting then
should be it's song
can you hear it's melody
over your cold and lonely war?

WHERE ARE YOU?

Where are you?
we used to play as children in the Sun
free to roam and run
but where are you?
I took that bully on our road of rocks
When you two fought in talks
So where are you?
We built great nations
Our own creations
We Fought dragons
Traveled through deserts in paddy wagons
Our adventures never lagging
In ferocity, formidity, and fatalities
How many times did we play dead
As our battles came to a head?
And we each bled with dread
That it was time for bed...
Battling, bargaining, and beseeching
But our time came to a halt
Silent, sudden, and screeching
Where did I lose?
When did you choose?
To leave and confuse?
Did I disjoint to the critical point
Of becoming an unrecognizable
And irreconcilable WHO....

To where now I scream....

WHERE ARE YOU?!

DESTINY

I'm going over and now it's easy to see
The days have bled into nights of horror.
Pensive sleep pulled purposely out parting my mind.
The hours burn by into misery and madness.
Seconds lasting days,
And days into weeks of futile features of
fake fronts for others to smile at.
I never said I would live forever
But my steps I've left behind shall show my winding
journey to this particular destiny.

THESE WILLOWS

These aged willows sway in a breeze coming
from below.
A breeze seeping from hell.
Can you consider that?
Can you feel that?
A gaping wound in the beautiful earth with an old
wooden staircase descending into absolute insanity.
This is my journey, and I fear that there will be no
staircase ascending back into reality.
But I'll give everything I have to find it.
Everything.
Every ounce of my beating heart.

WHAT DREAMS DO LIE

Shadows and hands
Whispers and cracks
There or Not?
Pray for Not....
But you hope all for Naught....

THOSE PRECIOUS FEW

They are the Lucky
those precious and few
that glide and soar
with perfect abandon
on stars aglow
and paths alight
Dare not I follow
with hopes in tow
and dreams forgot
I cannot see
through shifting sands
that mark my plight

THE WORLD JUST LOST IT'S BRIGHTEST LIGHT

Dear Uncle Russ,

   I want to say right off the top that I am going to miss you more than can be imagined or conceived of by my mind. I cannot fathom this world without your eternal spark of Joy that you have been to me ever since I was big enough for you to pick up and throw me into the deep end of the pool....laughing at me the whole time.

But all the while ready to leap in for the save had I ever needed it; but BECAUSE of you.....
I NEVER needed that save.

Because you taught me how to fight and survive the toss into the deep end....

No matter how deep it got.

It was simply IMPOSSIBLE not to smile whenever you were in the room.

I can still see you hollering and waving that University of Texas Cowbell every time we scored on "'Dem Damn Aggies".

I can feel your hand swatting down my attempt at a free throw shot on our dirt "Basketball Court" out in the backyard; and then lifting me up in the air to assist me in a Bad-Ass dunk.

I remember traveling home from Ft. Benning after completing Infantry Basic and pulling up to my grandparents place; where you had driven to, on your own, JUST to see me and tell me how incredibly proud you were.

That HUGE Uncle Russell smile on your face; always ready to brighten up the room and lift up the mood should it be called for.

I can recall you "Booty Dancing" with my bride at my wedding. How ridiculous you looked and how much laughter could be heard over the music as you put a smile on the face of anyone watching.

Regardless of the bad ending to that marriage story.....

Your dance moves, and the life you brought to the party, are memories I will cherish to the end of my days.

I love you Uncle Russ.
And you will be so desperately missed.

I'll be listening for that Cowbell buddy.
Love you.

ONLY IN WORDS

It was to be
  A Beautiful composition
  the forever spring
  from which we drew
Our tender beginnings
  that softly rendered
  such intimate poetry
  of the love we knew
Each moment you touched
  of our mortal eternity
  burned ever the brighter
  my simmering moon
So now our time
  so precious
  unspoken and perfect
  blazed too quickly
  and weathered too soon
Now I find myself here
  this vast chamber of empty
  the endless after,
  of our forever,
  where broken
  I weep
For the winter within
  that has swallowed my Fire
  and for the absence of light
  lost in the deep...

My fault...My fault...

My fault

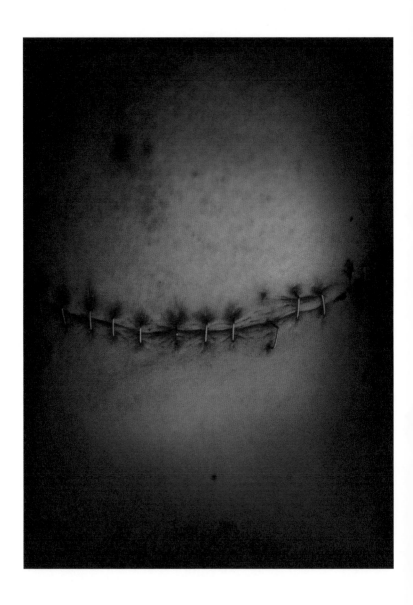

AWAKENED INSANITY

I am awake
Uncertain of how I arrived
Within these spiraled walls
Of leaking gore
My mind assaulted
And unable to understand
These lidless eyes
that smile and bore
Into my being
And soul within
I feel it's ghastly
And ghoulish gaze
Then to my horror
There appeared a mouth
Sagging and limp
To complete this face
Slowly and sounding
With succulent sips
Jagged teeth protruded
From runny flesh
In glee and holy terror
The slurping chasm
Of this mouth
Opened to my reeling distress
SLLAAAAUURRRPPPP!!!
It Screamed
And coughed about
These grotesque intestinal boils
That upon the slightest touch
Rupture and spit fire
On the unlucky few
Cursed to walk
These infinite toils.

YOUR OWN HERO

I know you know.
I know that you know how it feels.
To be that last piece.
The puzzle, put together so perfectly, lays upon your
table in it's completed Beauty.
Yet somehow......
a final piece lays off to the side;
ugly in it's fragmented loneliness.
Where does it go?
If the picture is final and ready to share...
What do you with the unwanted oddity?
Where the hell does it belong?
What should you do.....with you?
I wanted to be the Hero of my own story.
I yearned to stand triumphant over my demons
and the darkness they bring...
But what can you do when the villain
in your own tale...is you?
Who is to blame,
when your own mind is set so strongly against you?

August 8, 2017

"Sometimes you get tired. Sometimes you can feel the solitude like a heavy cloak weighing you down under water. Which makes the small random 'I love you's' that come out of no where that much more powerful and appreciated. So thank you."

-Daniel

HELP

Please help me
I need your hands
this day which followed
yesterday's shadow
has hastened my misery
and set my oblivion
I know not
what light there is
or darkness for time untold
yet I smile
a false chameleon
here I offer both
outstretched and open
in the hopes of your love
and in the hopes of your heart
where else can I go
this enormous anguish
that follows my steps
now conquers all
and ends at the start

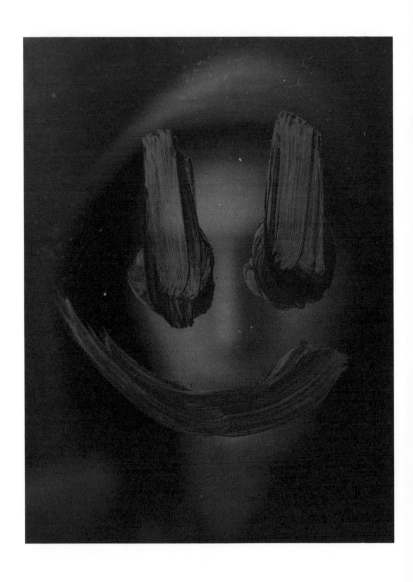

FAKING LAUGHTER

Shapeless terrors
damnation and all
How can you smile,
When should thee but Fall?
Shrieking
Reaching
Clawing
they howl,
wanting your thoughts
vulgar and foul.

MY GOD

-DEAR FATHER-

I think you hate me.
I believe it's because I embarrass you.
Don't we all feel that way about
the shit we've messed up in our lives?
Don't we all resent our MISTAKES?
And that's what I am....right?
When you get down to it...?
Past the pain...
And past the rage of it all?
Why should you love...
Why would you love...
Or be proud of
The utter and complete failure
That I am.
Why would you ever want me?
A MISTAKE.

Made in your image
But loathed in your heart.
A MISTAKE.

WITH ME

Will someone please walk with me?
Turn on the lights and dance with me?
Play the music and sing with me?
I need this now
more than ever before,
Because what I see in their eyes
has me casting to the floor.

I DON'T BELIEVE

I don't believe in Magic
I don't believe in Dreams
I don't believe good always wins
Or that Evil always sins

I don't believe in hoping
that things get better soon
they don't
they won't
they never will
bubonic promises overfill

I don't believe that there is good in everyone.
I don't believe there is someone looking out for us.
I don't believe in people anymore.
I don't believe that there is love for everyone.
I don't believe the worst is over.
I don't believe that we are meant to be happy.
I don't believe in us.
I don't believe we're born to do something.
I don't believe.
In anything.
Anymore.

DIMMING STARS

I feel small when i scream at the stars
Their endless lights fail to light my path
And I feel broken when I breathe
This shattered stone trail
Cuts and tears at my feet
And all I want is to leave
Trees yawn menacingly overhead
Darkening the way through these woods
And I trip falling to my knees
I lay there on my back
Covered in sickening mud of my blood
As the night presses weighted to tease
My escape from these razored leaves

SMALL

How small do you feel?
In comparison to this life lived....
How small do you feel?
Where have you been?
Where have you gone?
Where will you be?
The goodbyes we say turn to dust.
What meaning can we give to passing pains
and anguished cries?
This is where we are, no matter our repetitive
prayers for deliverance.
So through the tunnels of weathered stone
and shaded prints our past regrets.....
We exist.
But fail to live.....
Or feel.....
Those false hopes of purpose and meaning,
just beyond our weakened grasp.
How small do you feel?
Because in defiance of all logic,
I tell you now...
You are worth the fight.
Even if I fail,
You still carry a Beautiful promise.
One meant to light the way for those who
come behind you....
The Promise of Life.
Even if small.

THE BROOK

I stand alone in it's current.
This bubbling brook of madness
flows freely between my feet
as I, motionless, feel it's pull.

Constant and carefully crafted
it's banks lean precariously
towards it's rushing flow

All that once was
now but a memory,
under it's path of destructive deviance.
When too shall I join,
it's unrelenting topography of tangled torture?

- THANK YOU -

Well Ladies and Gentlemen,

That is it and we have reached the end of this particular journey.

I would like to thank each and every single one of you for making the effort and taking the time out of your personal lives to read all of these poems that I have put my heart and soul into over several years of writing.

This experience has been incredible and y'all purchasing this book and reading my words means the absolute world to me. So thank you.

I also want to take a moment to thank my very close and dear friend of mine who put so much work into putting this book together. Thank you.

To my parents, who pushed me to read and read and read, thank you for nourishing my love for literature.

And to my incredible supporters and friends; thank you for your boutiful love and compassion. It is because of y'all, and your countless requests for a collection of my poems, that truly made this dream project a reality.

Thank you.
From my heart.
Thank you.

FOLLOW THE AUTHOR ON SOCIAL MEDIA:

Instagram.com/danonepveux
@danonepveux

YouTube.com - Daniel Nepveux

Scan QR Code to go Daniel's YouTube Channel

Photo Credits:

Pg. 5 - Photography by Justus Menke on Unsplash.com

Pg. 7 - Photography by Tony Mucci on Unsplash.com

Pg. 9 - Photography by Valentin Salja on Unsplash.com

Pg. 11 - Photography by Camilo Jimenez on Unsplash.com

Pg. 13 - Photography by Rainer Krienke on Unsplash.com

Pg. 15 - Photography by Silver Ringvee on Unsplash.com

Pg. 17 - Photography by Daniel Lincoln on Unsplash.com

Pg. 19 - Photography by Raychel Sanner on Unsplash.com

Pg. 23 - Photography by Oliver Hihn on Unsplash.com

Pg. 25 - Photography by Daniele Levis on Unsplash.com

Pg. 27 - Photography by Mr. Xerty on Unsplash.com

Pg. 29 - Photography by Daniele Levis on Unsplash.com

Pg. 31 - Photography by Aviv Rachmadian on Unsplash.com

Pg. 33 - Photography by Nathan Wright on Unsplash.com

Pg. 35 - Photography by Alex Motoc on Unsplash.com

Pg. 37 - Digital art by Erin O'Neal

Pg. 41 - Photography by Francisco Andreotti on Unsplash.com

Pg. 43 - Photography by Ian on Unsplash.com

Pg. 47 - Photography by Daniel Nepveux

Pg. 49 - Photography by Cristian Newman on Unsplash.com

Pg. 51 - Photography by Robson Hatsukami Morgan on Unsplash

Pg. 53 - Photography by Marc Olivier Jodoin on Unsplash.com

Pg. 55 - Photography by David Holifield on Unsplash.com

Pg. 59 - Photography by Mat Reding on Unsplash.com

Pg. 61 - Photography by Carolyn V on Unsplash.com

Pg. 63 - Photography by Ante Samarzija on Unsplash.com

Pg. 65 - Photography by Chester Wade on Unsplash.com

Pg. 67 - Wilde, Oscar. *The Canterville Ghost*. Wilder
        Publications, 2018.

Pg. 69 - Photography by Jack B on Unsplash.com

Pg. 71 - Photography by Krists Luhaers on Unsplash.com

Pg. 73 - Quote from WTM, "The Mind's Journal"

Pg. 75 - Image from www.pixaby.com

Pg. 77 - Photography by Tyler Donaghy on Unsplash.com

Pg. 81 - Photography by Ian on Unsplash.com

Pg. 83 - Photography by Kamil Pietrzak on Unsplash.com

Photo Credits:

Pg. 85 - *Captain America: The First Avenger*. Directed by Joe Johnston. Produced by Marvel Studios. Distributed by Paramount Pictures. 2011
Pg. 87 - Photograph by Daniel Nepveux
Pg. 91 - *The Grey*. Directed by Joe Carnahan. Produced by LD Entertainment. Distributed by Open Road Films. 2012
Pg. 91 - Photography by Isai Ramos on Unsplash.com
Pg. 95 - Photography by Boba Jovanovic on Unsplash.com
Pg. 97 - Photography by Kelly Evans on Unsplash.com
Pg. 99 - Photography by Daniel Tuttle on Unsplash.com
Pg. 101 - Photography by Ante Hamersmit on Unsplash.com
Pg. 103 - Photography by Hayley Catherine on Unsplash.com
Pg. 105 - Photography by Kreated Media on Unsplash.com
Pg. 109 - Photography by Irmaweb on Pixabay.com
Pg. 111 - Photography by Sharon McCutcheon on Unsplash.com
Pg. 113 - Photography by Ryoji Iwata on Unsplash.com
Pg. 117 - Photography by Teslariu Mihai on Unsplash.com
Pg. 119 - Photography by Joshua Earle on Unsplash.com
Pg. 121 - Photography by Annie Spratt on Unsplash.com
Pg. 123 - Photography by Dave Babler on Unsplash.com
Pg. 125 - Photography byMichael Liao on Unsplash.com
Pg. 127 - Photography by Matti Keponen on Unsplash.com
Pg. 129 - Photography by Vincent Foret on Unsplash.com

Printed in Great Britain
by Amazon